Alfred's Basic Piano Library

Chord Approach

A PIANO METHOD FOR THE LATER BEGINNER

Lesson Book
LEVEL 1

FOREWORD

ALFRED'S BASIC CHORD APPROACH provides an alternate beginning to piano study especially designed for the student aged 10 or older, when the hands are strong enough to begin the use of three-note chords. In the regular series, three-note chords are not presented until late in Level 2 (the third book of the series, since this is preceded by Levels 1A and 1B).

In the CHORD APPROACH, the student begins to play three-note chords on page 26 of Level 1. This allows the use of fuller harmonies for the pieces. It should be carefully noted, however, that chords are introduced only after the hands have been adequately prepared by playing melodic and harmonic 2nds, 3rds, 4ths and 5ths. This preparation also enables the student to thoroughly understand the intervalic formation of the chords.

The pieces in the CHORD APPROACH series have been carefully selected to appeal to students for the ages recommended. Some material has been borrowed from the Alfred Fun Books, and a few of the favorite selections from the regular course have been retained, but most material used is completely different than that found in the regular Alfred's Basic Piano Library, Levels 1A, 1B & 2. These books will, therefore, serve as an answer to the problem of needing different materials for use by two students of different ages in the same family.

Although the CHORD APPROACH books progress more rapidly than the regular 1A, 1B & 2 Levels, there are no gaps, and there are plenty of overlaps to insure a thorough understanding of each concept introduced. Additional material for reinforcing each concept will be found in the Solo, Theory, Technic, Duet and Christmas books prepared for use with the CHORD APPROACH Lesson Books 1 and 2. After completing the two levels of the CHORD APPROACH books, the student continues to the regular Level 3 books of Alfred's Basic Piano Library.

© *Copyright MCMLXXXVII by Alfred Publishing Co., Inc.*

2

Contents

How to Sit at the Piano

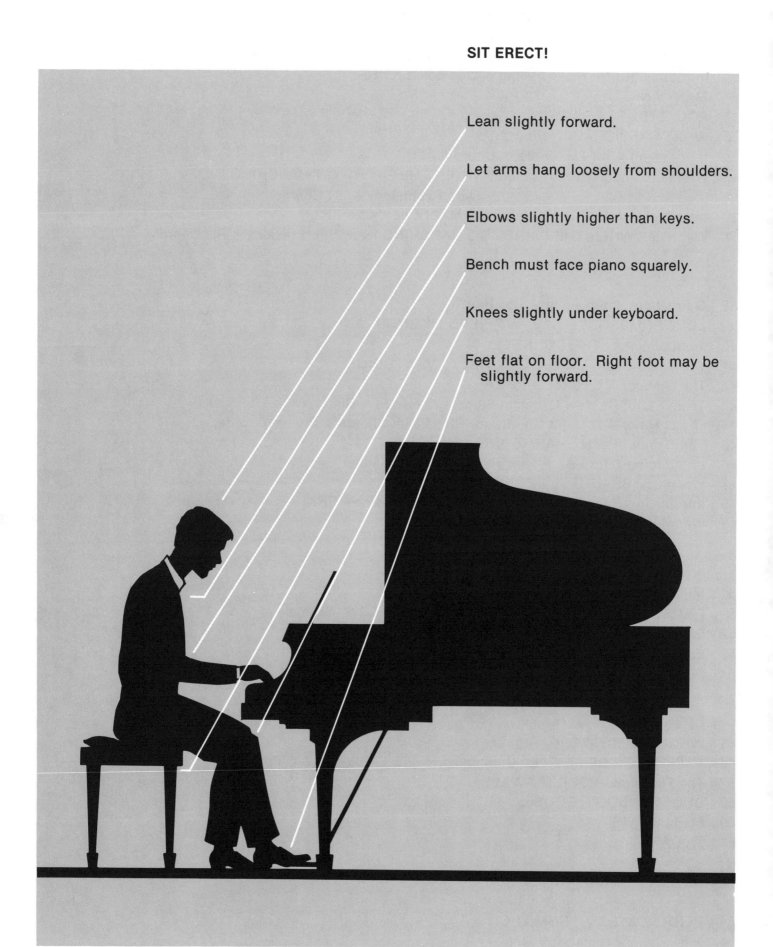

SIT ERECT!

Lean slightly forward.

Let arms hang loosely from shoulders.

Elbows slightly higher than keys.

Bench must face piano squarely.

Knees slightly under keyboard.

Feet flat on floor. Right foot may be slightly forward.

How Fingers Are Numbered

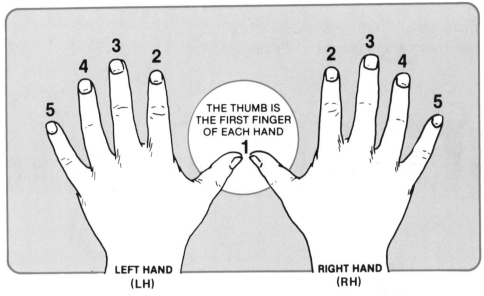

THE THUMB IS THE FIRST FINGER OF EACH HAND

LEFT HAND (LH)

RIGHT HAND (RH)

Before you begin to play, practice moving each finger
as you say its number aloud.

How Piano Tones Are Made

When you play a key, a hammer inside your piano touches a string to make a tone.
When you drop into a key with a LITTLE weight, you make a SOFT tone.
When you use MORE weight, you make a LOUDER tone.

String

Hammer

Curve your fingers, because:

- Fingers are different lengths, but when you curve them they can touch the keys as if their lengths were the same.
- The thumb cannot reach the keys unless the other fingers are curved.
- The keys respond more quickly and easily when fingers are curved.

Pretend you have a bubble in your hand.

Hold the bubble gently, so it doesn't break!

1. Play any white key with the 3rd finger of either hand, softly.
2. See how many times you can repeat the same key, making each tone a little louder.

Before you play any key you should always decide how soft or loud you want it to sound.

For the first pieces in this book, play with a MODERATELY LOUD tone.

The Keyboard

The keyboard is made up of white keys and black keys.
Notice that the black keys are in groups of 2's and 3's.

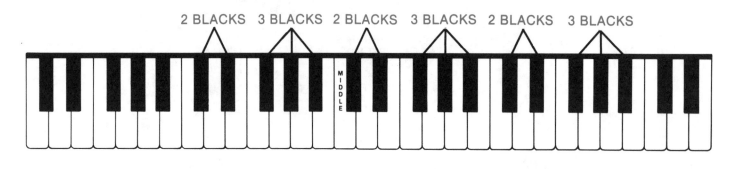

2 BLACKS   3 BLACKS   2 BLACKS   3 BLACKS   2 BLACKS   3 BLACKS

LOW SOUNDS ← LEFT IS **DOWN** (Lower)   RIGHT IS **UP** (Higher) → **HIGH SOUNDS**

Play the 2 BLACK KEY groups!

LH

1. Using L H 2 3, begin at the middle and play all the 2 black key groups going ← DOWN the keyboard (both keys at once).

2. Using R H 2 3, begin at the middle and play all the 2 black key groups going UP → the keyboard (both keys at once).

RH

3. Repeat, without looking at your hands.

Play the 3 BLACK KEY groups!

LH

4. Using L H 2 3 4, begin at the middle and play all the 3 black key groups going ← DOWN the keyboard (all 3 keys at once).

5. Using R H 2 3 4, begin at the middle and play all the 3 black key groups going UP → the keyboard (all 3 keys at once).

RH

6. Repeat, without looking at your hands.

Naming the Keys

Piano keys are named for the first seven letters of the alphabet, beginning with **A.**

A B C D E F G

Each white key is recognized by its position in or next to a black key group!

For example: **A**'s are found between the **TOP TWO KEYS** of each **3 BLACK KEY GROUP.**

Play the following. Use LH 3 for keys below the middle of the keyboard.
Use RH 3 for keys above the middle of the keyboard.

Say the name of each key aloud as you play!

Play all the A's
on your piano.

Play all the B's.

Play all the C's.

Play all the D's.

Play all the E's.

Play all the F's.

Play all the G's.

It is easy to name every white key on your piano!

The key names are **A B C D E F G,** USED OVER AND OVER.

The LOWEST key
on your piano
is **A.**

The C nearest the
middle of the piano
is called **MIDDLE C.**

Going **UP** the keyboard, the notes sound **HIGHER and HIGHER!**

Play and name every white key beginning with bottom A.

Use LH 3 for keys below middle C, and RH 3 for keys above middle C.

You are now ready to begin Chord Approach THEORY BOOK, Level 1.

The Treble Staff

Music is written on a STAFF of 5 lines and 4 spaces.

Music for the RIGHT HAND is
written on the TREBLE STAFF,
identified by the TREBLE CLEF SIGN  which came from the letter "G."

Middle C is written on a short line below the staff, called a *leger* line. D is written higher,
on the space below the staff. Each next higher note is written on the next higher line or space.

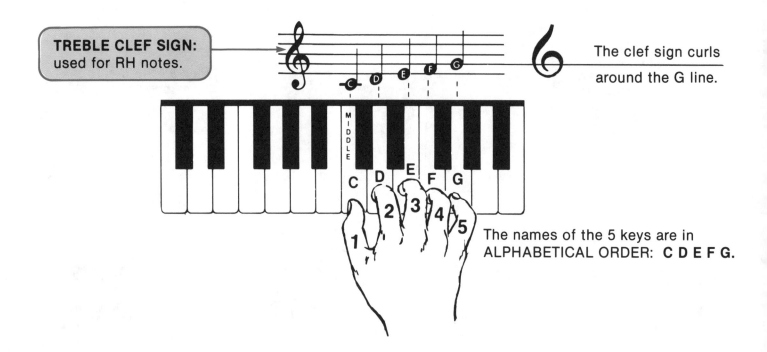

TREBLE CLEF SIGN:
used for RH notes.

The clef sign curls

around the G line.

The names of the 5 keys are in
ALPHABETICAL ORDER: **C D E F G.**

RH C Position

Place the RIGHT HAND in the above position. Keep the fingers curved and relaxed.

Play the following *WARM-UP.* Say the name of each note aloud as you play.
Repeat until you can play smoothly and evenly. As the notes go higher on the keyboard,
they are written higher on the staff!

Fingers:

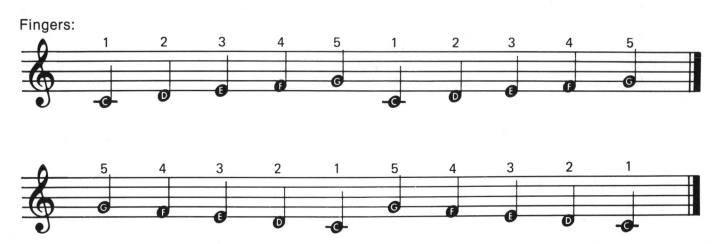

Quarter Notes & Half Notes

Music is made up of **short** tones and **long** tones. We write these tones in **notes**,
and we measure their lengths by **counting**. The combining of notes into patterns is called RHYTHM.

Quarter Note

a **short** note.

COUNT: "1"
or: "Quarter"

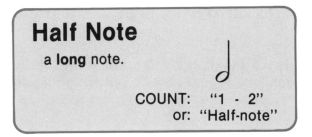

Half Note

a **long** note.

COUNT: "1 - 2"
or: "Half-note"

Clap (or tap) the following rhythm. Clap ONCE for each note, counting aloud.
Notice how the BAR LINES divide the music into MEASURES of equal duration.

ODE TO JOY

(Theme from Beethoven's 9th Symphony)

1. Clap (or tap) the rhythm evenly, counting aloud.
2. Play and sing (or say) the finger numbers.
3. Play and count.
4. Play and sing (or say) the note names.

Fingers:

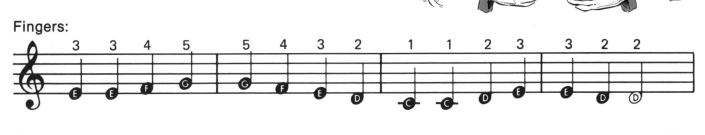

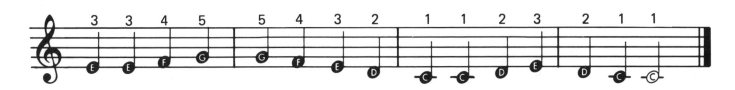

The Bass Staff

Music for the LEFT HAND is written on the BASS STAFF.
The bass staff also has 5 lines and 4 spaces.

It is identified by the BASS CLEF SIGN which came from the letter "F."

C is written on the 2nd space of the staff.
Each next higher note is written on the next higher line or space.

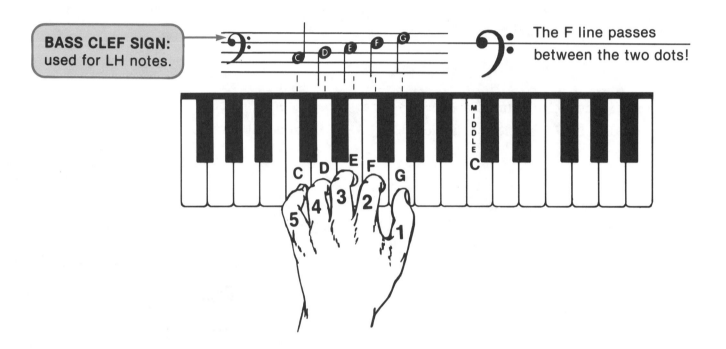

LH C Position

Place the LEFT HAND in the above position. Keep the fingers curved and relaxed.

Play the following *WARM-UP.* Say the name of each note aloud as you play.
Repeat until you can play smoothly and evenly.

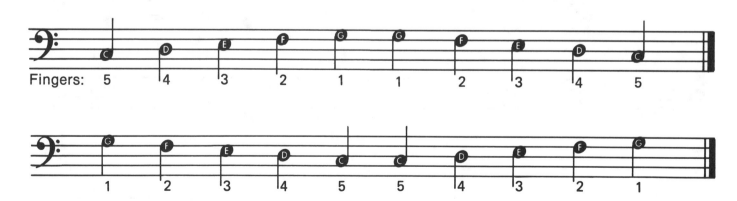

When notes are BELOW the MIDDLE LINE of the staff, the stems usually point UP.
When notes are ON or ABOVE the MIDDLE LINE, the stems usually point DOWN.

The Whole Note

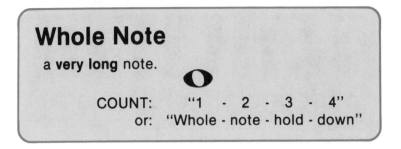

Whole Note

a **very long** note. 𝅝

COUNT: "1 - 2 - 3 - 4"

or: "Whole - note - hold - down"

Clap (or tap) the following rhythm. Clap **ONCE** for each note, counting aloud.

ROW, ROW, ROW YOUR BOAT

(RIGHT SIDE UP AND UPSIDE DOWN)

The 1st line is the familiar tune.
The 2nd line is the same, upside-down!

1. Clap (or tap) the rhythm, counting aloud.
2. Play and sing (or say) the finger numbers.
3. Play and count.
4. Play and sing (or say) the note names.

This is a good procedure to follow for each piece or exercise you play.

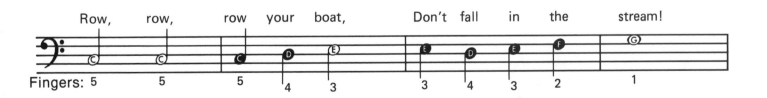

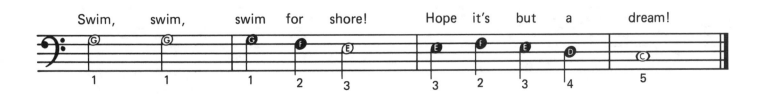

The Grand Staff

The BASS STAFF & TREBLE STAFF, when joined together with a BRACE, make up the **GRAND STAFF.**

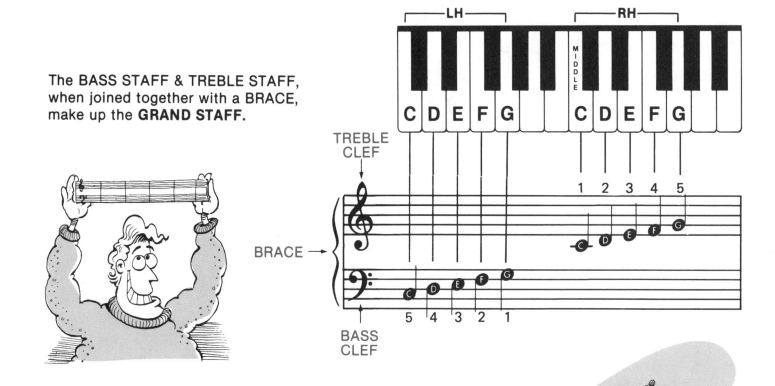

PLAYING ON THE GRAND STAFF

Only the starting finger number for each hand is given.

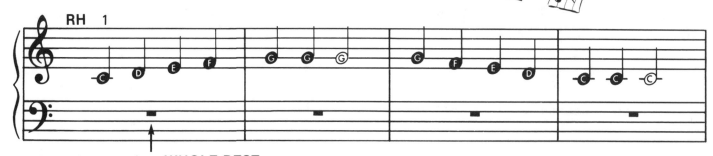

This sign 𝆩 is a **WHOLE REST.**
LH is silent a whole measure!

RH silent a whole measure.

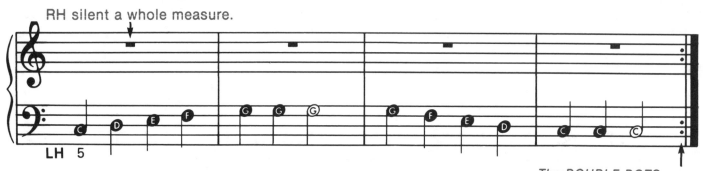

The DOUBLE DOTS mean REPEAT FROM THE BEGINNING.

The Time Signature

Music has numbers at the beginning called the **TIME SIGNATURE**.
The **TOP NUMBER** tells the number of beats (counts) in each measure.
The **BOTTOM NUMBER** tells the kind of note that gets ONE beat (count).

4 = **4** beats to each measure.

4 = **QUARTER NOTE** ♩ gets ONE beat.

	NOTE	COUNT	TOTAL NUMBER OF COUNTS
QUARTER	♩	"1"	1
HALF	♪	"1 - 2"	2
WHOLE	𝅝	"1 - 2 - 3 - 4"	4

Note-Reading Made Easy!

Find the starting note. If the next note is on the same line or space, play the same key again. If the note moves UP on the staff, play a higher key. If the note moves DOWN on the staff, play a LOWER key.

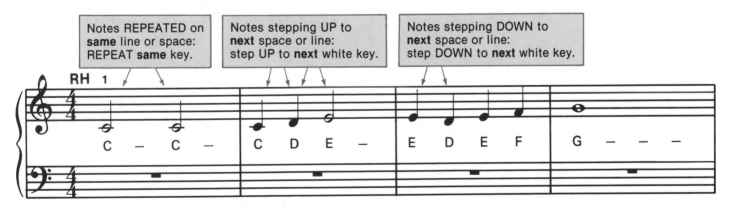

Note-reading is very easy if you remember that the notes on the staff are like a picture of the way the fingers move on the keys.

You are now ready to begin Chord Approach DUET BOOK, Level 1.

Measuring Distances in Music

Distances from one note to another are measured in INTERVALS, called 2nds, 3rds, etc.

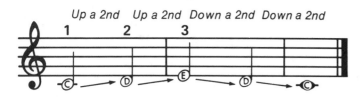 The distance from any white key to the next white key, up or down, is called a 2nd.

> 2nds are written LINE-SPACE or SPACE-LINE.

Play, saying "UP a 2nd," etc.

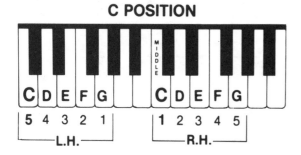

C POSITION

SLUR:  or

SLURS mean play LEGATO.
LEGATO means SMOOTHLY CONNECTED.

SECONDS

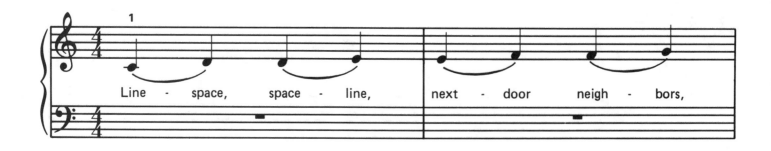

Line - space, space - line, next - door neigh - bors,

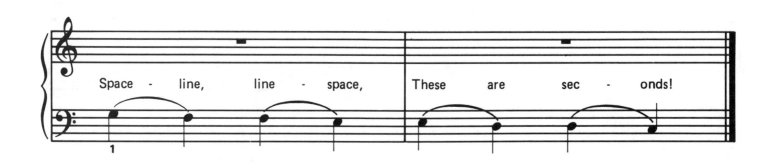

Space - line, line - space, These are sec - onds!

GLIDING

DYNAMIC SIGNS tell how LOUD or SOFT to play.

mf (mezzo forte) = *MODERATELY LOUD*

Moderately slow

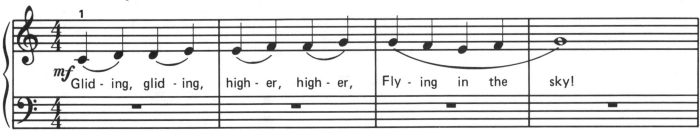

mf Glid - ing, glid - ing, high - er, high - er, Fly - ing in the sky!

Glid - ing, glid - ing, low - er, low - er, What a way to fly!

mf

DUET PART: (Student plays 1 octave higher.)

Moderately slow

mf   RH   LH

New Time Signature

Dotted Half Note

3/4 means **3** beats to each measure.
a **quarter note** gets one beat.

Dotted Half Note
a **longer** note.
COUNT: "1 - 2 - 3"

C POSITION

1. Clap (or tap) the following rhythm.
2. Clap **ONCE** for each note, counting aloud.

STRANGE LANDS

SLURS often divide the music into PHRASES.
A PHRASE is a musical thought or sentence.

Moderately slow

mf

1. Strange lands beck - on to me,
2. Strange sounds ring in to my ear,

Lands I'm long - ing to see.
Sounds I'm long - ing to hear.

mf

DUET PART: (Student plays 1 octave higher.)

Moderately slow

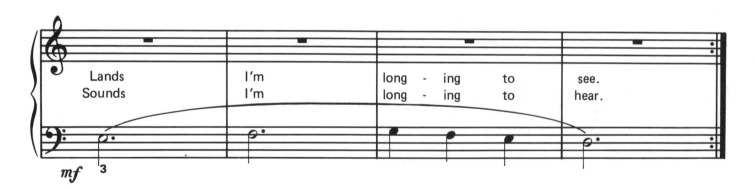

RH

LH

p

You are now ready to begin Chord Approach TECHNIC BOOK, Level 1.

1. Clap (or tap) the following rhythm.
2. Clap **ONCE** for each note, counting aloud.

MY WISH

p (PIANO) = SOFT

Moderately slow

1. If my dreams could all come true,
2. For the things I'd like to do,

I would make a wish or two,
And I'd save a wish for you.

DUET PART: (Student plays 1 octave higher.)

Moderately slow

Intervals: 3rds

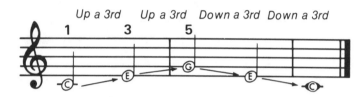 When you skip a white key, the interval is a 3rd.

3rds are written LINE-LINE or SPACE-SPACE.

Play, saying "UP a 3rd," etc.

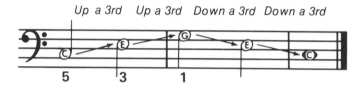

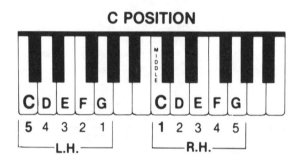

C POSITION

C D E F G | C D E F G
5 4 3 2 1 | 1 2 3 4 5
L.H. | R.H.

THIRDS

Moderately slow

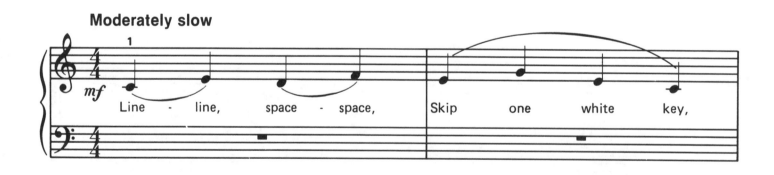

mf

Line - line, space - space, Skip one white key,

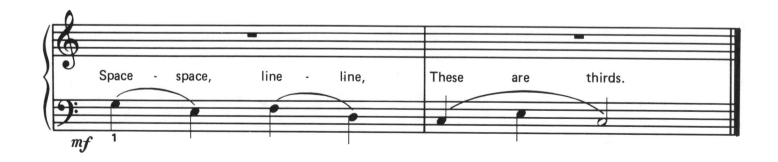

Space - space, line - line, These are thirds.

mf

JOIN THE FUN

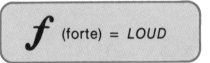

f (forte) = *LOUD*

Moderately fast

Ev - 'ry - one join the fun. Come and hear the mu - sic play!

Join the fun, ev - 'ry - one. Let's have fun to - day.

DUET PART: (Student plays 2 octaves higher.)

Moderately fast

Melodic Intervals

Notes played **SEPARATELY** make a **MELODY**.
We call the intervals between these notes **MELODIC INTERVALS**.

Play these MELODIC 2nds & 3rds. Listen to the sound of each interval.

Find all the melodic 2nds and 3rds in the following pieces before you play.

AU CLAIRE DE LA LUNE

Moderately slow

TISKET, A TASKET

Moderately fast

You are now ready to begin Chord Approach SOLO BOOK, Level 1.

Harmonic Intervals

Notes played **TOGETHER** make **HARMONY**.

We call the intervals between these notes **HARMONIC INTERVALS**.

Play these HARMONIC **2nds** & **3rds.** Listen to the sound of each interval.

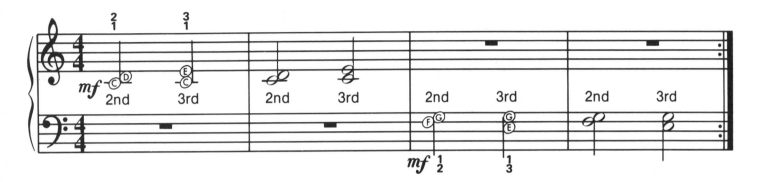

ROCKIN' INTERVALS

This sign is a **QUARTER REST.**
Rest for one count!

Brightly

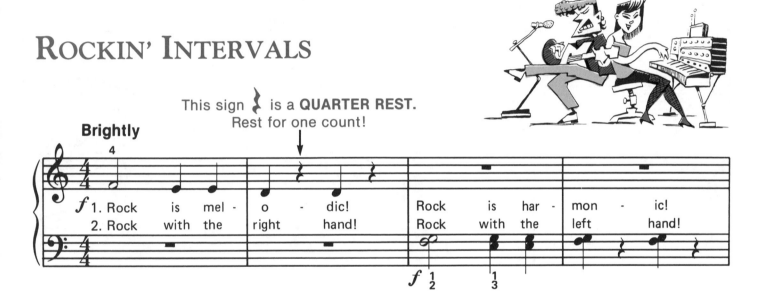

1. Rock is mel - o - dic! Rock is har - mon - ic!
2. Rock with the right hand! Rock with the left hand!

Rock is mel - o - dic! Rock is har - mon - ic!
Rock with the right hand! Rock with the left hand!

DUET PART: (Student plays 1 octave higher.)

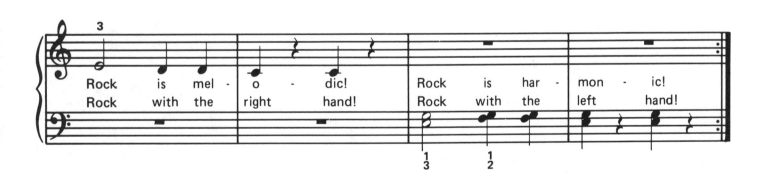

Intervals: 4ths

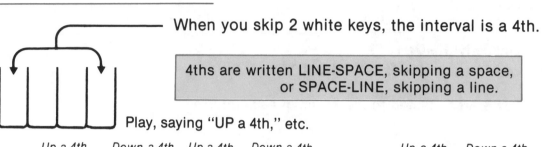

When you skip 2 white keys, the interval is a 4th.

4ths are written LINE-SPACE, skipping a space,
or SPACE-LINE, skipping a line.

Play, saying "UP a 4th," etc.

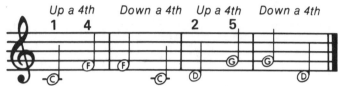

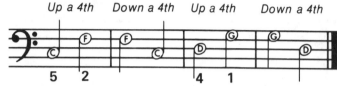

MELODIC FOURTHS

Moderately slow

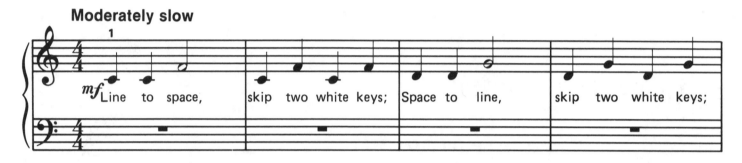

Line to space, skip two white keys; Space to line, skip two white keys;

Space to line, line to space, That's the way to play a fourth!

AURA LEE

This folk melody was made into a popular song, "LOVE ME TENDER," sung by Elvis Presley.

Moderately slow

Intervals: 5ths

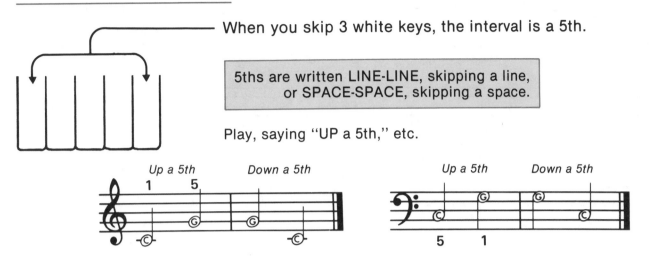

When you skip 3 white keys, the interval is a 5th.

5ths are written LINE-LINE, skipping a line,
or SPACE-SPACE, skipping a space.

Play, saying "UP a 5th," etc.

MELODIC FIFTHS

Moderately slow

mf Line to line, skip three white keys; Up a fifth! Down a fifth!

Space to space, skip three white keys; Up a fifth! Down a fifth!

mf

ROCK ALONG!

Moderately fast

f Play thirds and fifths, and we'll rock a - long!

f Just thirds and fifths for a good rock song!

Harmonic Fourths & Fifths

Play these HARMONIC **4ths** & **5ths**. Listen to the sound of each interval.

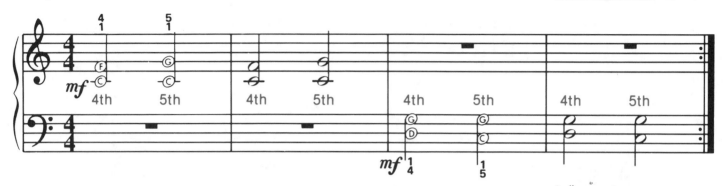

JINGLE BELLS

Before you play: 1. Find all the MELODIC 4ths & 5ths in the RH.
2. Find all the HARMONIC 4ths & 5ths in the LH.

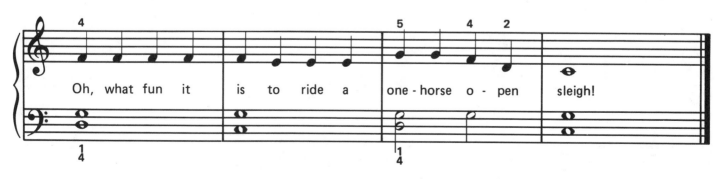

Interval Review

MELODIES

This piece reviews melodic 2nds, 3rds, 4ths & 5ths.

Name all the MELODIC INTERVALS in this piece before you play it.

HARMONIES

This piece reviews harmonic 2nds, 3rds, 4ths & 5ths.

Name all the HARMONIC INTERVALS in this piece before you play it.

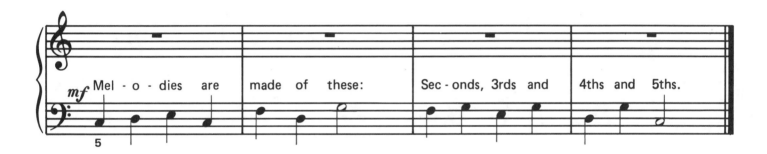

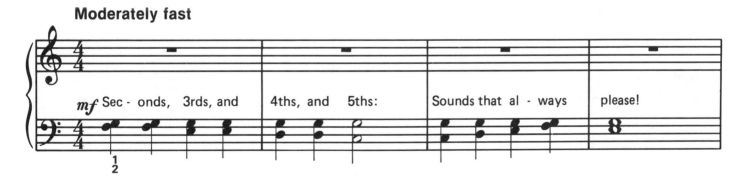

The C Major Chord

A chord is three or more notes played together.

The **C MAJOR CHORD** is made of three notes: **C E G.**

C is called the **ROOT** of the chord. The chord gets its letter-name from the ROOT.
E is called the **3rd** of the chord. It is a 3rd above the ROOT.
G is called the **5th** of the chord. It is a 5th above the ROOT.

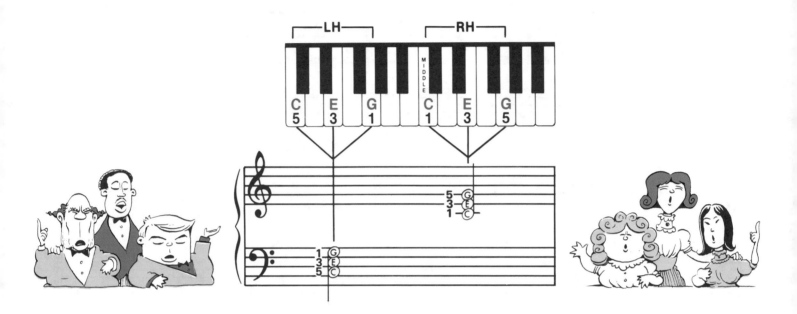

Be sure to play all three chord notes exactly together, with fingers nicely curved.

C MAJOR CHORDS for LH

Play & count.

C MAJOR CHORDS for RH

Play & count.

BROTHER JOHN

READ BY PATTERNS! For RH, think:
"C, up a 2nd, up a 2nd, down a 3rd," etc.
THINK the pattern, then PLAY it!

Moderately fast

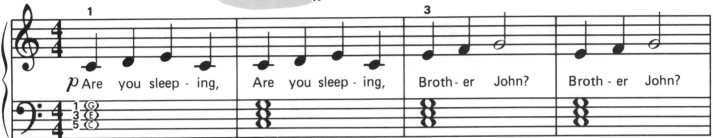

Are you sleep-ing, Are you sleep-ing, Broth-er John? Broth-er John?

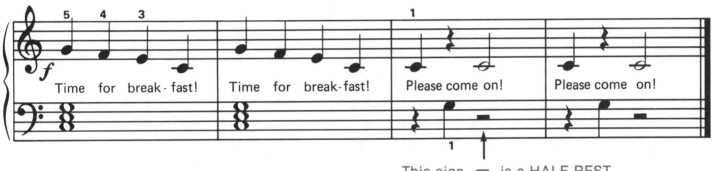

Time for break-fast! Time for break-fast! Please come on! Please come on!

This sign ▬ is a HALF REST.
Rest for two counts!

THE ONE-MAN BAND

READ BY PATTERNS! For LH, think:
"E, same, same, down a 3rd, up a 3rd," etc.

Moderately fast

I'm just like a one-man band! Songs to you I bring.

I play rhy-thm, I play chords; I play ev-'ry-thing!

Introducing (B) for Left Hand

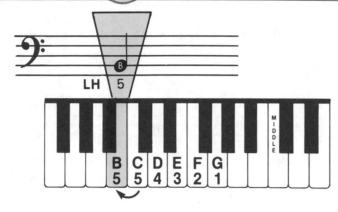

TO FIND B:

Place the LH in **C POSITION.** Reach finger 5 one white key to the left!
Play slowly. Say the note names as you play.

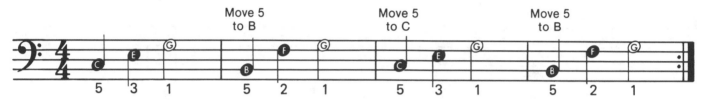

C Major & G⁷ Chords for Left Hand

Two frequently used chords are **C MAJOR** & **G⁷.** For ease in playing, the notes of the G⁷ chord presented here are B F G, an interval of a 5th and a 2nd. The chord gets its letter-name from the root G—the top note of the interval of the 2nd.*

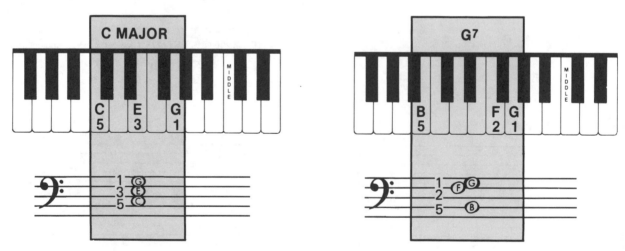

Practice changing from the C major chord to the G⁷ chord and back again:
1. The 1st finger plays G in both chords.
2. The 2nd finger plays F in the G⁷ chord.
3. Only the 5th finger moves out of C POSITION (down to B) for G⁷.

*NOTE TO TEACHERS: The G⁷ chord is formed by adding a 7th (F) to the G major chord. For ease in playing, the 3rd (B) & 7th (F) are lowered one octave; the 5th (D) is omitted. The formation of the 7th chord will be fully explained in Level 2.

TIED NOTES: When notes on the *same* line or space are joined with a curved line, we call them **TIED NOTES.**

The key is held down for the
COMBINED VALUES OF BOTH NOTES!

COUNT: "1 - 2 - 3 - 4,　　1 - 2 - 3 - 4."

MERRILY WE ROLL ALONG

Play the RH & LH separately at first, then together.
Practice the RH **mf** and the LH **p**.
The melody should always be clearly heard above the accompaniment.

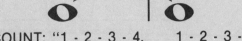

(TIED NOTES!)

LARGO *(from "THE NEW WORLD")*

This melody is also known as *GOING HOME.*

Dvorak

Introducing Ⓑ for Right Hand

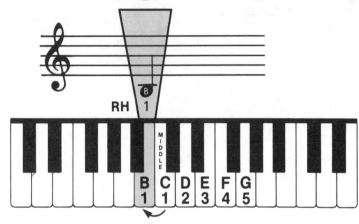

RH

TO FIND B:

Place the RH in **C POSITION**.
Reach finger 1 one white key to the left!

Play slowly. Say the note names as you play.

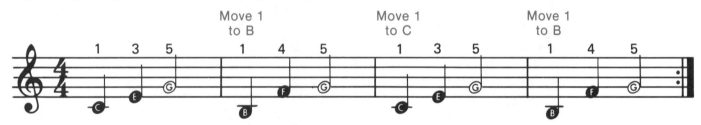

Move 1 to B   Move 1 to C   Move 1 to B

C Major & G⁷ Chords for Right Hand

It is very important to be able to play all chords with the RIGHT hand as well as the LEFT. Chords are used in both hands in popular and classical music.

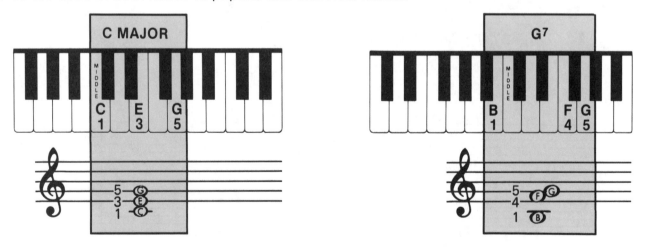

Practice changing from the C major chord to the G⁷ chord and back again:

1. The 5th finger plays G in both chords.
2. The 4th finger plays F in the G⁷ chord.
3. Only the 1st finger moves out of C POSITION (down to B) for G⁷.

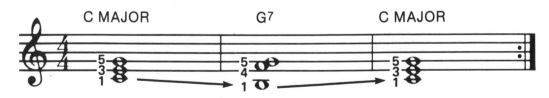

C MAJOR   G⁷   C MAJOR

MARY ANN

Calypso tune

Moderately fast

All day, all night, Ma-ry Ann, (Ma-ry Ann,)

Down by the sea-shore, sift-in' sand; (sift-in' sand;)

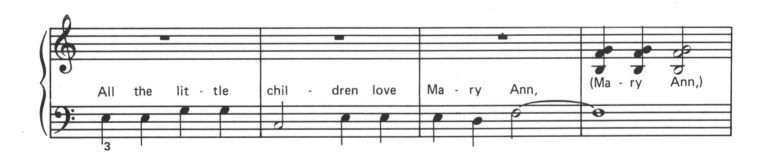

All the lit-tle chil-dren love Ma-ry Ann, (Ma-ry Ann,)

Down by the sea-shore sift-in' sand. (sift-in' sand.)

ROCKETS

C major & G⁷ chords in LH.

Moderately fast

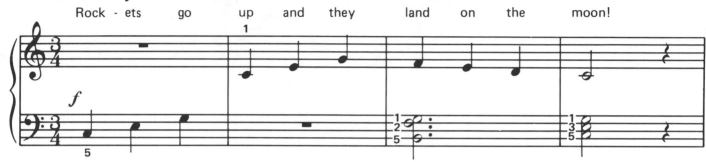

Rock - ets go up and they land on the moon!

Rock - ets will trav - el to oth - er worlds soon!

IMPORTANT! Play *ROCKETS* again, playing the 2nd line one octave (8 notes) higher.
The rests at the end of the 1st line give you time to move your hands to the new position!

SEA DIVERS

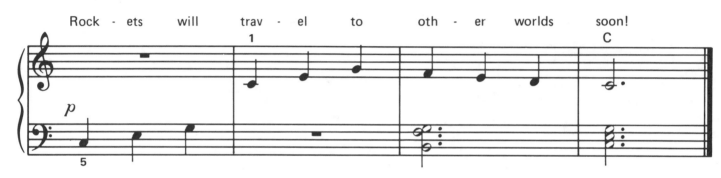

C major & G⁷ chords in RH.

Moderately slow

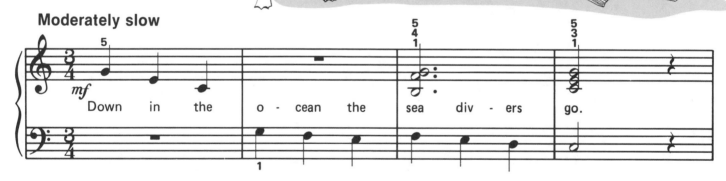

Down in the o - cean the sea div - ers go.

May - be they'll find man - y treas - ures be - low!

IMPORTANT! Play *SEA DIVERS* again, playing the 2nd line one octave lower.

REMEMBER: SLURS mean play LEGATO (smoothly connected).
Slurs often divide the music into PHRASES.
A PHRASE is a musical sentence.

WHAT CAN I SHARE?

Moderately slow

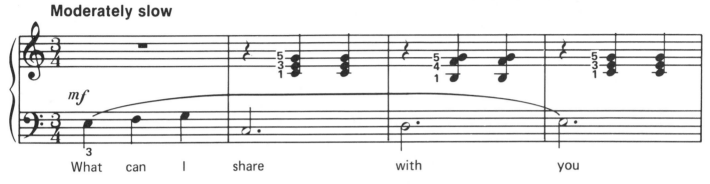

What can I share with you

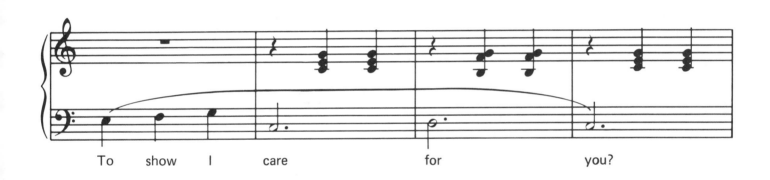

To show I care for you?

Good friends should al ways share

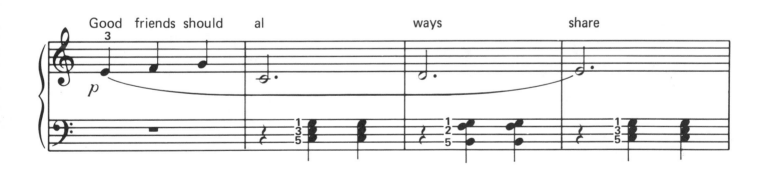

To show how much they care!

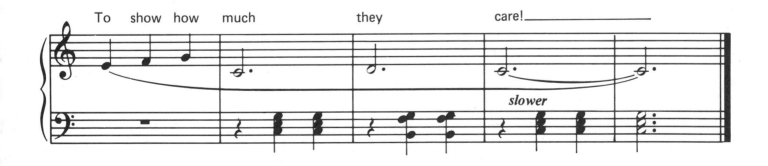

slower

Introducing (A) for Left Hand

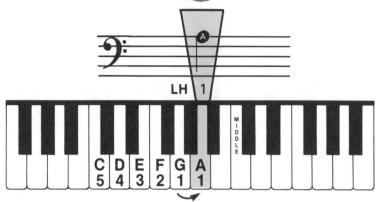

TO FIND A:

Place the LH in **C POSITION.**
Reach finger 1 one white key to the right!

Play slowly. Say the note names as you play.

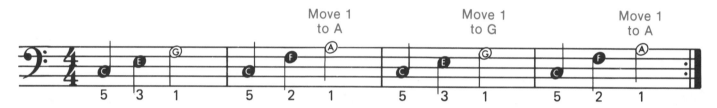

The F Major Chord for Left Hand

The C MAJOR chord is frequently followed by the F MAJOR chord. For smooth playing, the notes of the F MAJOR chord presented here are C F A, an interval of a 4th and a 3rd. The chord gets its letter-name from the root F—the top note of the interval of the 4th.

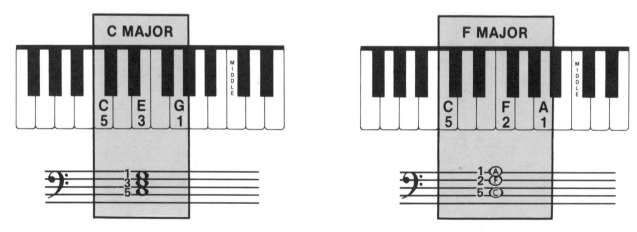

Practice changing from the C major chord to the F major chord and back again.

1. The 5th finger plays C in both chords.
2. The 2nd finger plays F in the F chord.
3. Only the 1st finger moves out of C POSITION (up to A) for the F chord.

Warm-up Using C Major, G⁷ & F Major Chords

Practice SLOWLY at first, then gradually increase speed.

INCOMPLETE MEASURE:

Some pieces begin with an INCOMPLETE MEASURE. The 1st measure of this piece has only 3 counts. The missing count is found in the last measure! When you repeat the whole song, you will have one whole measure of 4 counts when you play the last measure plus the first measure.

WHEN THE SAINTS GO MARCHING IN

(With RH MELODY & LH CHORDS)

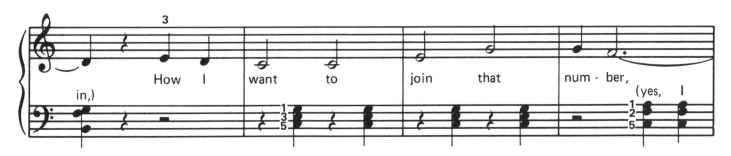

Introducing  A for Right Hand

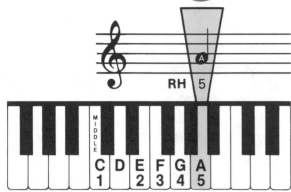

TO FIND A:

Place the RH in **C POSITION.**
Leave 1 on C.
Shift all other fingers one white key to the right!

Play slowly. Say the note names as you play.

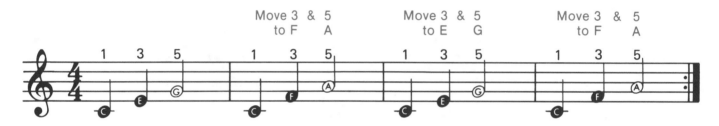

C Major & F Major Chords for Right Hand

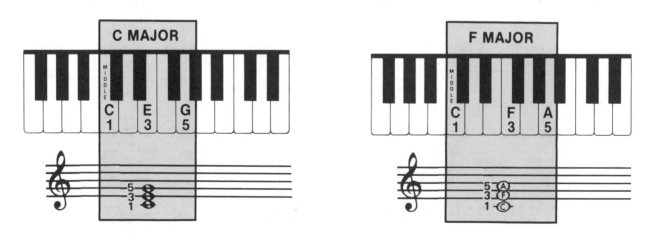

Practice changing from the C major chord to the F major chord and back again:
1. The 1st finger plays C in both chords.
2. The 3rd finger moves up to F and the 5th finger moves up to A for the F chord.

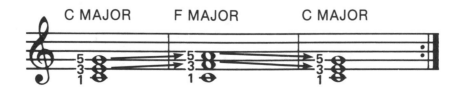

Warm-up Using C Major, G⁷ & F Major Chords

WHEN THE SAINTS GO MARCHING IN

(With LH MELODY & RH CHORDS)

March time

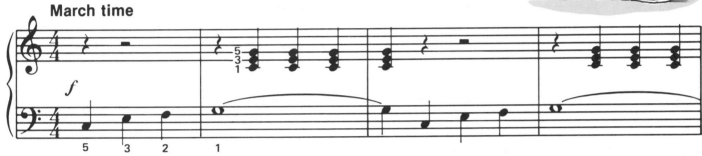

After you have learned both versions of *WHEN THE SAINTS GO MARCHING IN,* you will find it very effective to play page 35 followed immediately by page 37. Instead of playing the piece one way and repeating, you will be playing the melody first in the RH, then in the LH!

G Position

Until now you have played only in the C POSITION.
Now you will move to the G POSITION:

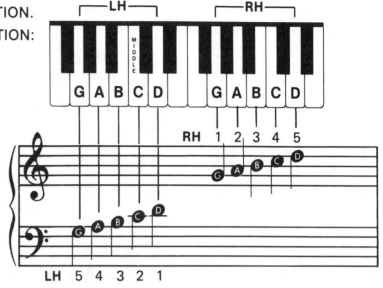

RH 1 on the G above middle C.

LH 5 on the G below middle C.

Play and say the note names. Be sure to do this **SEVERAL TIMES!**

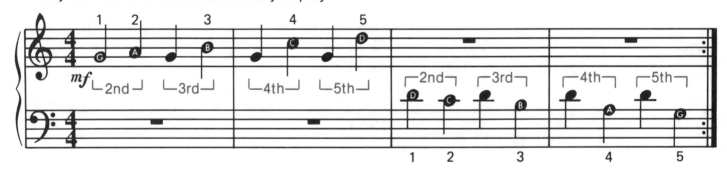

Intervals in G Position

1. MELODIC INTERVALS

Say the name of each interval as you play.

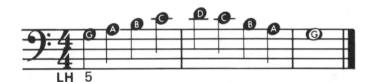

2. HARMONIC INTERVALS

Say the name of each interval as you play.

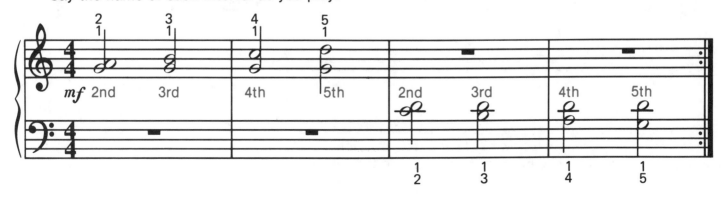

LOVE SOMEBODY!

G POSITION

Before playing hands together, play LH alone, naming each harmonic interval!

Happily

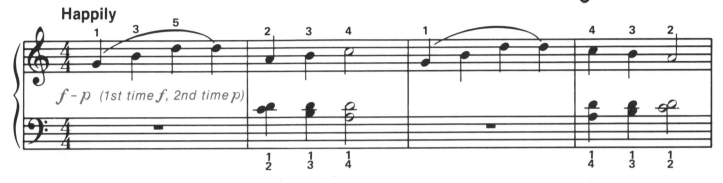

A FRIEND LIKE YOU

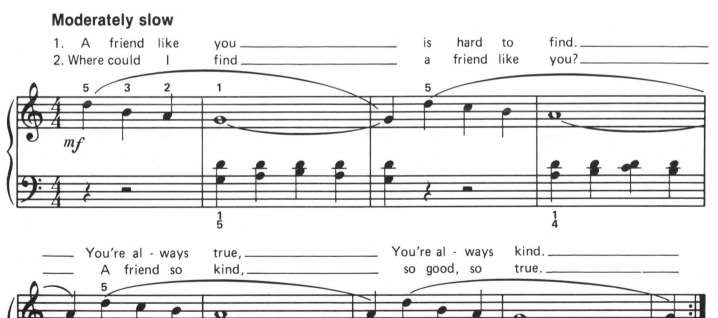

G POSITION

Before playing hands together, play LH alone, naming each harmonic interval!

Moderately slow

1. A friend like you _____ is hard to find. _____
2. Where could I find _____ a friend like you?

_____ You're al - ways true, _____ You're al - ways kind. _____
_____ A friend so kind, _____ so good, so true. _____

*Repeat with LH
one octave (8 notes) lower.*

Tempo Marks

TEMPO is an Italian word. It means "RATE OF SPEED."
Words indicating the rate of speed used in playing music
are called **TEMPO MARKS.**

Here are some of the most important tempo marks:

    ALLEGRO = Quickly, happily.
    MODERATO = Moderately.
    ANDANTE = Moving along. The word actually means "walking."
    ADAGIO = Slowly.

THE DONKEY

G POSITION

Before playing hands together, play LH alone, naming each harmonic interval.

Allegro moderato (Moderately fast)

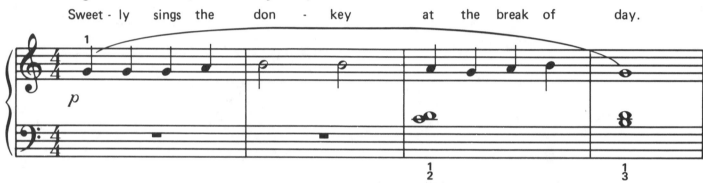

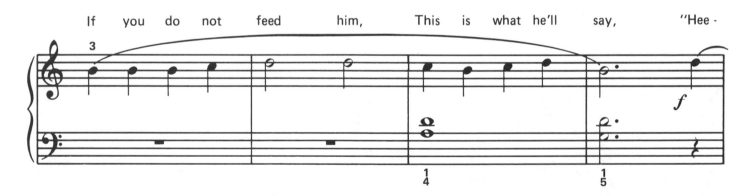

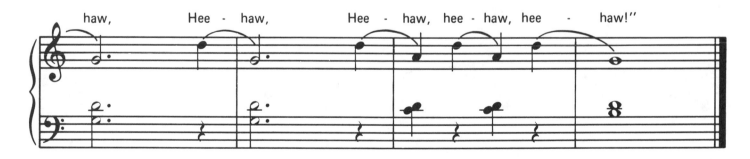

THE DONKEY may be played as a ROUND for 2 to 4 pianos. The 2nd piano begins after the 1st has played 4 measures. The 3rd begins after the 2nd has played 4 measures, etc. Play 4 times.

The Sharp Sign

The **SHARP SIGN** before a note means play the next key to the RIGHT, whether black or white!

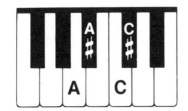

When a SHARP (♯) appears before a note, it applies to that note for the rest of the measure!

Circle the notes that are SHARP:

MONEY CAN'T BUY EV'RYTHING!

G POSITION

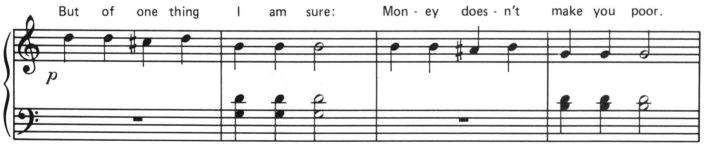

March tempo

Mon - ey can't buy ev - 'ry - thing! Mon - ey can't make you a king.

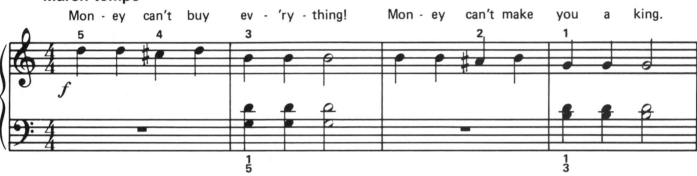

Mon - ey may not bring suc - cess; Mon - ey can't buy hap - pi - ness!

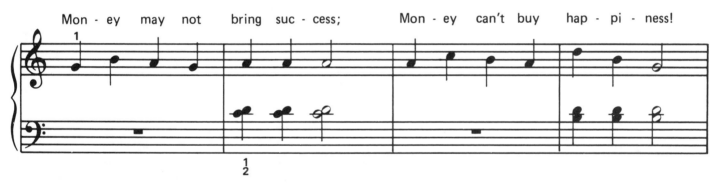

But of one thing I am sure: Mon - ey does - n't make you poor.

Mon - ey does - n't make you sad; Mon - ey can't be all that bad!

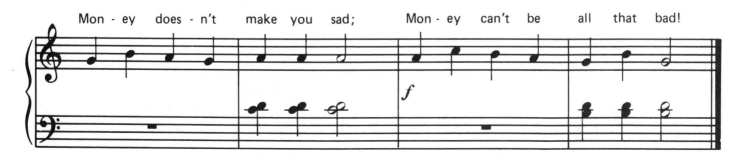

G Major & D⁷ Chords for Left Hand

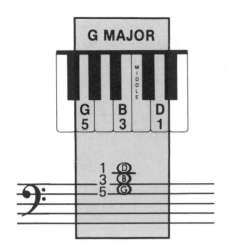 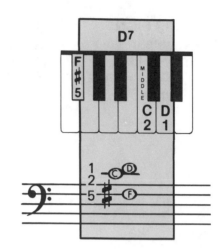

Practice changing from the G major chord to the D⁷ chord and back again:

1. 1 plays D in both chords.
2. 2 plays C in the D⁷ chord.
3. Only 5 moves out of G POSITION (down to F♯) for D⁷.

Play the following several times.

Preparation for *THE CUCKOO.*

THE CUCKOO

G POSITION

NEW DYNAMIC SIGNS

CRESCENDO (gradually louder)   **DIMINUENDO** (gradually softer)

G Major & D⁷ Chords for Right Hand

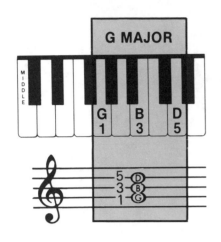 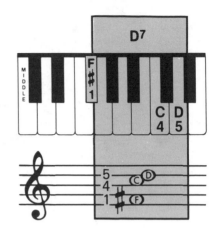

Practice changing from the G major chord to the D⁷ chord and back again:

1. 5 plays D in both chords.
2. 4 plays C in the D⁷ chord.
3. Only 1 moves out of G POSITON (down to F♯) for D⁷.

Play several times:

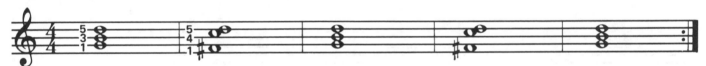

Block Chords and Broken Chords

When all three notes of a chord are played together, it is called a BLOCK CHORD.
When the three notes of a chord are played separately, it is called a BROKEN CHORD.

Play several times:

The Damper Pedal

The RIGHT PEDAL is called the **DAMPER PEDAL.**

When you hold the damper pedal down, any tone you sound
will continue after you release the key.

Use the RIGHT FOOT on the damper pedal.
Always keep your heel on the floor. Use your ankle like a hinge.

This sign means: PEDAL DOWN   PEDAL UP

⌐ ——————————— HOLD PEDAL ——————————— ⌐

HARP SONG

G POSITION

Many pieces are made entirely of broken chords, as this one is!
Identify all G major & D⁷ chords before you play.

Adagio moderato (Moderately slow)

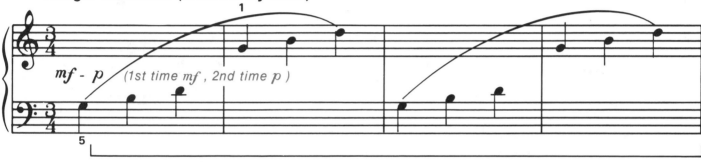

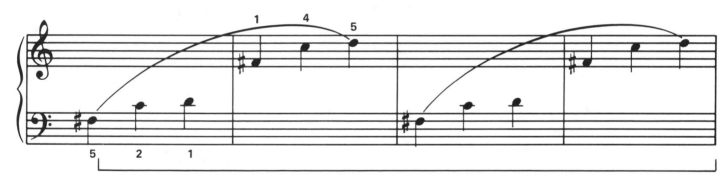

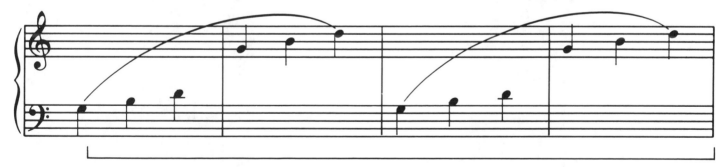

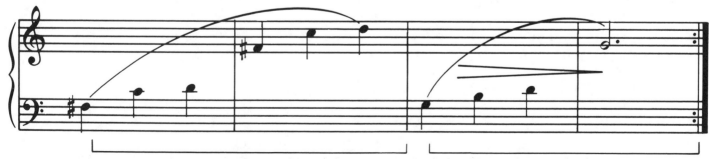

Also play *HARP SONG* in the following ways:

1. Play the 3rd & 4th measures of each line one octave higher than written.
2. Play the 1st & 2nd measures of each line one octave lower than written.

Introducing (E) for Left Hand

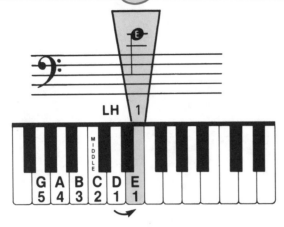

TO FIND E:

Place the LH in **G POSITION**.
Reach finger 1 one white key to the right!

Play slowly. Say the note names as you play.

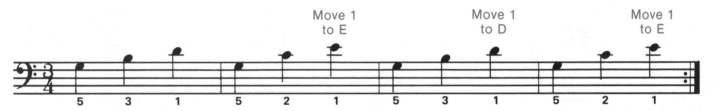

Move 1 to E   Move 1 to D   Move 1 to E

A New Position of the C Major Chord

You have already played the C MAJOR CHORD with C as the lowest note: that is **C E G**.
When you play these same 3 notes in any order, you still have a C MAJOR CHORD.
When you are playing in G POSITION, it is most convenient to play G as the lowest note: **G C E.**

The following diagrams show how easy it is to move from the G MAJOR CHORD to the
C MAJOR CHORD, when G is the lowest note of both chords.

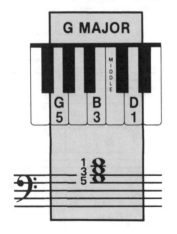

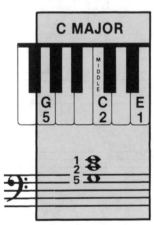

Practice changing from the G major chord to the C major chord and back again:

1. 5 plays G in both chords.
2. 2 plays C in the C chord.
3. Only 1 moves out of G POSITION (up to E) for the C chord.

G MAJOR   C MAJOR   G MAJOR

Warm-up Using G Major, D⁷ & C Major Chords

This warm-up introduces a new way of playing BROKEN CHORDS.

BEAUTIFUL BROWN EYES

Introducing (E) for Right Hand

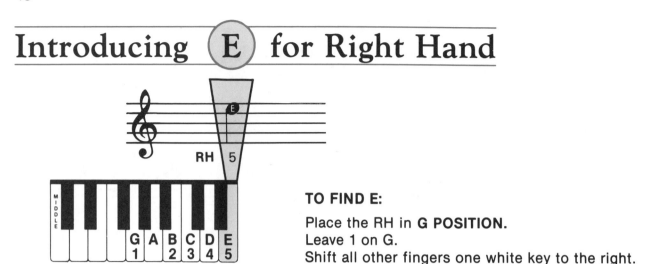

TO FIND E:

Place the RH in **G POSITION.**
Leave 1 on G.
Shift all other fingers one white key to the right.

Play slowly. Say the note names as you play.

New C Major Chord Position—Right Hand

Notice that TWO fingers must move to the right when changing from the G MAJOR CHORD to the C MAJOR CHORD.

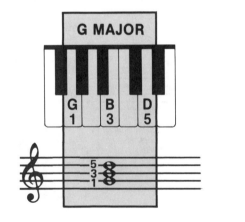

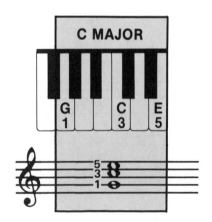

Practice changing from the G major chord to the C major chord and back again:
1. 1 plays G in both chords.
2. 3 moves up to C and 5 moves up to E for the C chord.

Warm-up Using G Major, D⁷ & C Major Chords

Play SLOWLY at first, then gradually increase speed.

JUST ONE MORE WALTZ!

The LH melody of this piece consists entirely of BROKEN CHORDS, which are the same as the BLOCK CHORDS played by the RH!

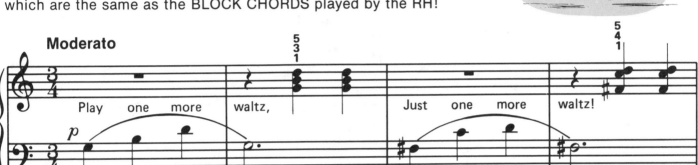

Play one more waltz, Just one more waltz!

Mom loves to waltz to the "Ten-nes-see Waltz."

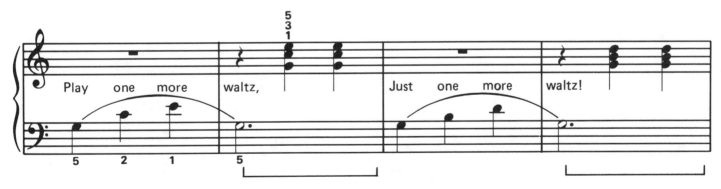

Play one more waltz, Just one more waltz!

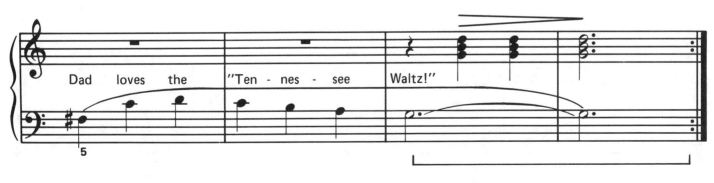

Dad loves the "Ten-nes-see Waltz!"

Middle C Position

The MIDDLE C POSITION uses notes you already know! The RH is in C POSITION,
and the LH moves one note down from the G POSITION! Both thumbs are now on Middle C.

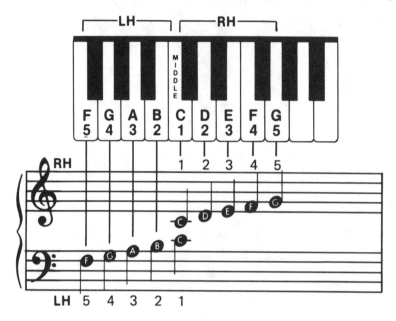

Play and say the note names. Do this several times!

THUMBS ON C!

Adagio moderato

PRAISE GOD, FROM WHOM ALL BLESSINGS FLOW

> This sign is called a **FERMATA**.
>
> Hold the note under the FERMATA longer than its value.

MIDDLE C POSITION

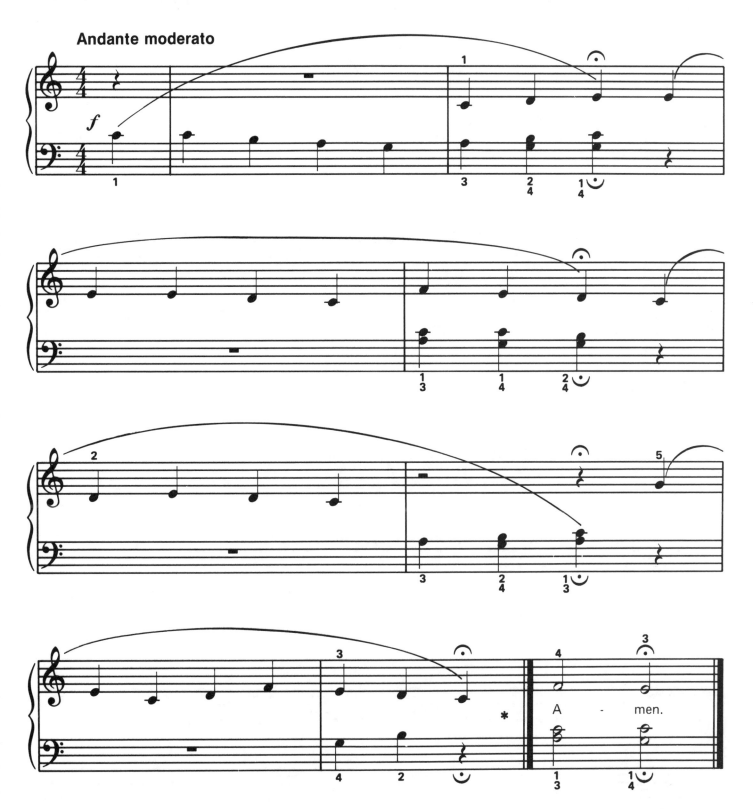

*When a hymn begins with an incomplete measure, the missing counts are found
in the last measure of the hymn itself. The AMEN is considered to be an added ending.

GOOD MORNING TO YOU!

MIDDLE C POSITION

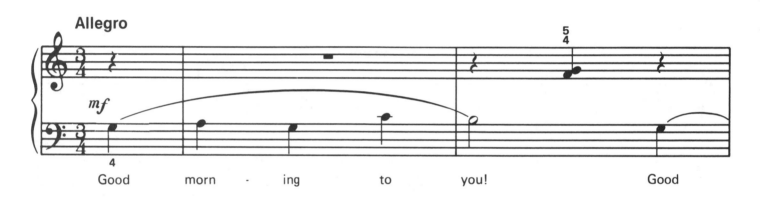

Good morn - ing to you! Good

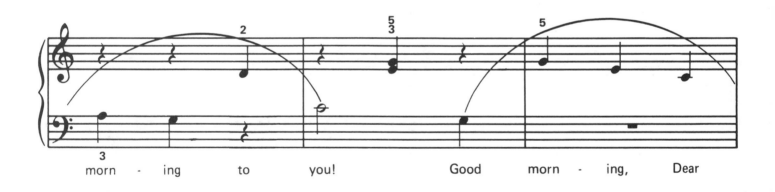

morn - ing to you! Good morn - ing, Dear

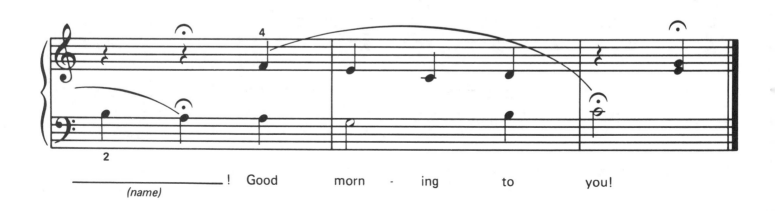

_____ ! Good morn - ing to you!
(name)

Eighth Notes

Two eighth notes are played in the time of **one quarter note.**

When a piece contains eighth notes,
count: "**1 · &**" or "**quar · ter**" for each quarter note;
count: "**1 · &**" or "**2 · 8ths**" for each pair of eighth notes.

Clap (or tap) these notes, counting aloud.

Eighth notes are usually played in **pairs.**
COUNT: "1 · &"
OR: "2 · 8ths"

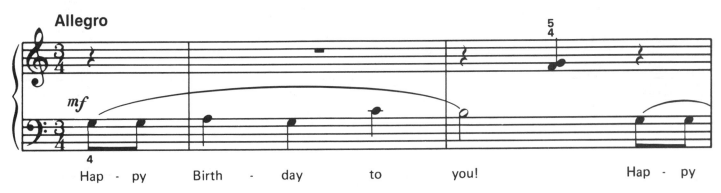

HAPPY BIRTHDAY TO YOU!

HAPPY BIRTHDAY is exactly the same as *GOOD MORNING TO YOU,* except for the EIGHTH NOTES!

Allegro

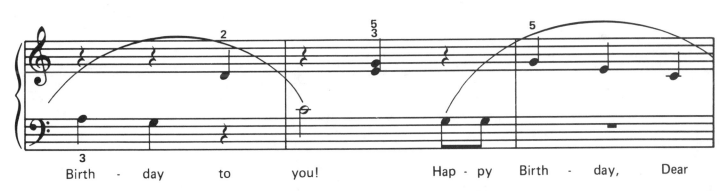

Hap - py Birth - day to you! Hap - py

Birth - day to you! Hap - py Birth - day, Dear

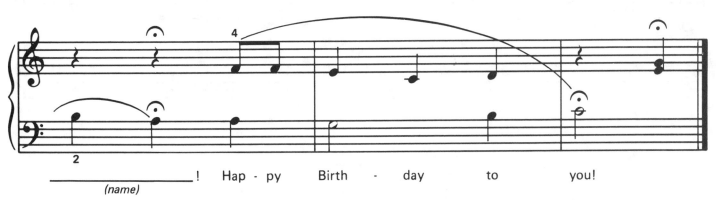

_____! Hap - py Birth - day to you!
(name)

For the Beauty of the Earth

MIDDLE C POSITION

Words by F. S. Pierpoint
Melody by Conrad Kocher

Adagio moderato

2. For the wonder of each hour
   Of the day and of the night,
   Hill and vale and tree and flower,
   Sun and moon, and stars of light:

   CHORUS

WHOOPEE TI-YI-YO

C POSITION

Cowboy song

Allegro moderato

f Whoop-ee ti - yi - yo, Get a - long, lit - tle do - gies, It's

your mis - for - tune and none of my own; Whoop-ee

ti - yi - yo, Get a - long, lit - tle do - gies, For you

know Wy - om - ing will be your new home!

*A "dogie" is an orphaned calf. The first syllable, "do," rhymes with "go."

THE GIFT TO BE SIMPLE

COMBINING MIDDLE C POSITION & C POSITION

You are now ready to play music that involves more than one position. This piece begins with the hands in MIDDLE C POSITION. After the first full measure is played, the LH moves to C POSITION to play chords. Change positions as indicated in the music.

This beautiful old Shaker melody was used by the famous American composer, Aaron Copland, in his well known symphonic composition, *Appalachian Spring.*

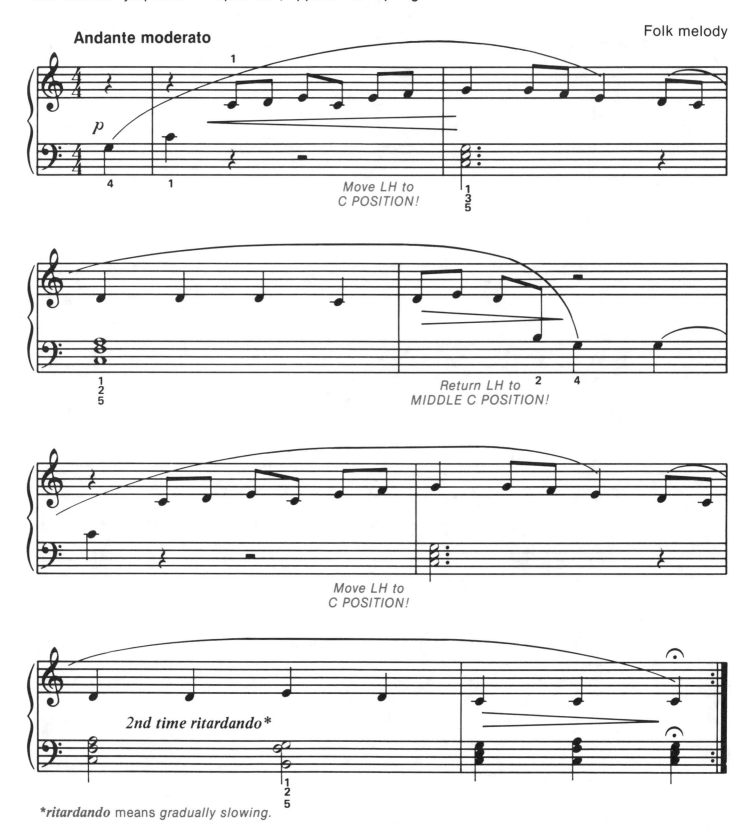

ritardando means *gradually slowing.*

The Flat Sign

The **FLAT SIGN** before a note means play the next key to the LEFT, whether black or white.

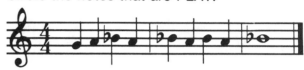

When a FLAT (♭) appears before a note, it applies to that note for the rest of the measure.

Circle the notes that are FLAT:

ROCK IT AWAY!

G POSITION

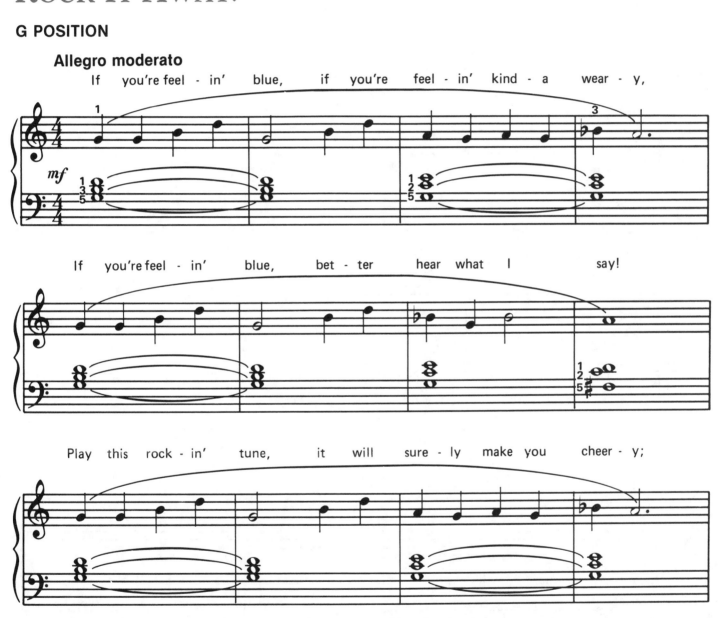

Allegro moderato

If you're feel-in' blue, if you're feel-in' kind-a wear-y,

mf

If you're feel-in' blue, bet-ter hear what I say!

Play this rock-in' tune, it will sure-ly make you cheer-y;

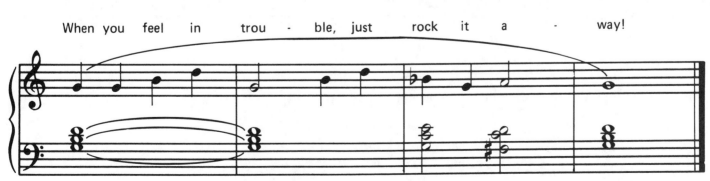

When you feel in trou-ble, just rock it a - way!

BOOGIE-WOOGIE GOOSE

C POSITION

REMEMBER: The sharp sign raises a note,
the flat sign lowers a note.

Allegro moderato

Go tell Aunt Rho - die,   Go tell Aunt

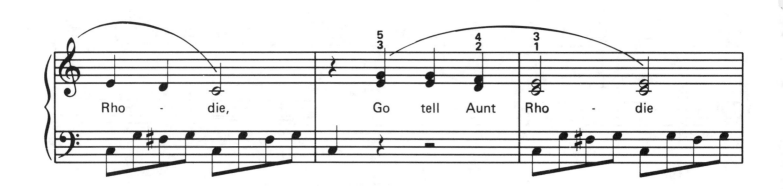

Rho - die,   Go tell Aunt Rho - die

* Pairs of eighth notes may be played a bit unevenly, in a "lilting" style:

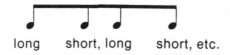

long   short, long   short, etc.

her goose is - n't dead.

f It's do - in' the boo - gie, It's do - in' the

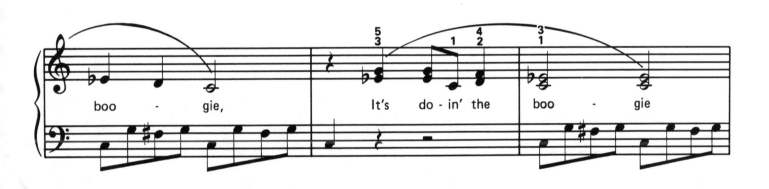

boo - gie, It's do - in' the boo - gie

in her flow - er bed! *ritardando*

FÜR LUDWIG*

C POSITION

Not too fast, but with great optimism

p If I prac - tice well, some - day you'll hear me

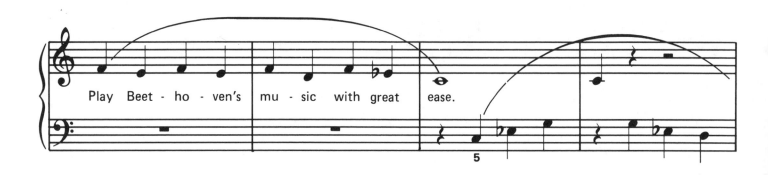

Play Beet - ho - ven's mu - sic with great ease.

If I prac - tice well, some - day you'll hear me

Play that mu - sic he wrote for E - lise.

ONE OCTAVE LOWER

*Ludwig van Beethoven—Composer of *Für Elise* (For Elise).

This is an **ACCENT SIGN.**

> When there is an ACCENT SIGN
over or under a note,
play that note LOUDER.

TA-DAH!

RH in G POSITION
LH in C POSITION

Allegro

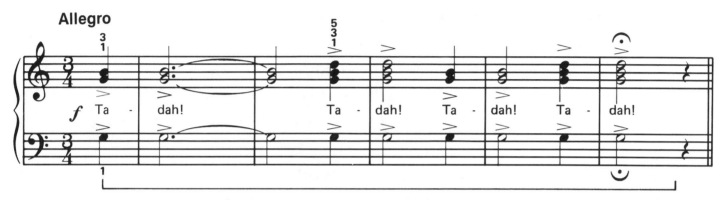

f Ta - dah! Ta - dah! Ta - dah! Ta - dah!

**With great pomp and power,
Not too slow!**

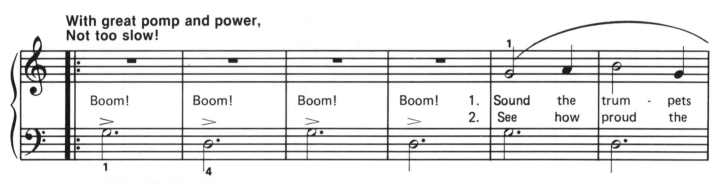

Boom! Boom! Boom! Boom!
1. Sound the trum - pets
2. See how proud the

LH ONE OCTAVE LOWER

here I come! Ring the bells and rat - tle the drum!
peo - ple look! Shake my hand, I fin - ished the book!

rit - - ard - - an - - do - - - - - - - - -

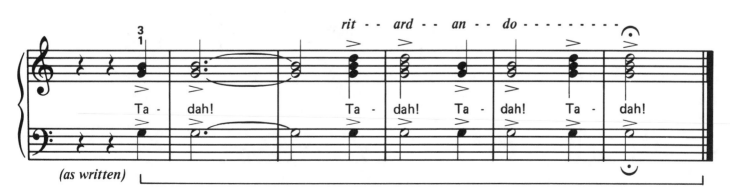

Ta - dah! Ta - dah! Ta - dah! Ta - dah!

(as written)

Review of Musical Terms

Accent (>)	placed over or under a note that gets special emphasis. Play the note louder.
Adagio	slowly.
Allegro	quickly, happily.
Andante	moving along (at walking speed).
Crescendo (◁————)	gradually louder.
Diminuendo (————▷)	gradually softer.
Dynamic signs	signs showing how loud or soft to play.
Fermata (⌒)	indicates that a note should be held longer than its true value.
Flat sign (♭)	lowers a note one half step. Play the next key to the left.
Forte (*f*)	loud.
f–p	1st time loud, 2nd time soft.
Harmonic interval	the interval between two tones sounded together.
Incomplete measure	a measure at the beginning of a piece with fewer counts than shown in the time signature. The missing counts are found in the last measure.
Interval	the difference in pitch (highness or lowness) between two tones.
Legato	smoothly connected. Usually indicated by a slur over or under the notes.
Melodic interval	the interval between two tones sounded separately.
Mezzo forte (*mf*)	moderately loud.
Moderato	moderately.
Pedal mark (└——————┘)	press the damper pedal, hold it, and release it.
Piano (*p*)	soft.
Repeat signs	repeat from the beginning.
Ritardando (abbreviated *ritard.* or *rit.*)	gradually slowing.
Sharp sign (♯)	raises a note one half step. Play the next key to the right.
Tempo	rate of speed.
Time signatures ($\frac{3}{4}$, $\frac{4}{4}$)	numbers found at the beginning of a piece or section of a piece. The top number shows the number of beats in each measure. The bottom number shows the kind of note that gets one beat.